Relief, Have You A Name?

poems by

Phoebe Marrall

From the collection of Jane Hendrickson and Camille Komine
Compiled and edited by Gayle Jansen Beede

Finishing Line Press
Georgetown, Kentucky

Relief, Have You A Name?

ACKNOWLEDGMENTS

From the collection of Jane Hendrickson and Camille Komine
Compiled and edited by Gayle Jansen Beede

This chapbook was made possible in part by donations to the ONE LAST WORD
Program. ONE LAST WORD helps to bring the last works of gifted poets to the
world.

Publisher: Leah Huete de Maines
FLP Editor: Christen Kincaid
Cover Art: Phoebe Marrall
Author Photo: Jane Hendrickson

Order online: www.finishinglinepress.com
also available on amazon.com

Author inquiries and mail orders:
Finishing Line Press
P. O. Box 1626
Georgetown, Kentucky 40324
U. S. A.

Table of Contents

Part Three

FOREWARD

A paper clip, abandoned rubber bands, the tail end of a ball of household string, discarded boxes of Tylenol, new and used No. 2 pencils, knitted patches of yarn—all have found their way into the art of Phoebe Marrall. Like Andy Warhol's *Campbell's Soup Cans* and *Brillo Boxes,* or the colorful contributions to the Pop Art genre of Sister Corita Kent, under whose tutelage Phoebe studied at Immaculate Heart College in Los Angeles, Marrall's artistic expressions celebrate, mirror, mime, and evoke the beauty of the everyday. Hers is truly *found* art.

A survivor of The Depression, and of child abuse, Phoebe learned to cope with her grueling childhood by embracing the potential, the usefulness, the beauty and grace of objects and creatures big and small. In her work, no insect deserves a death sentence; even a cobweb holds mystique. Breath is not something you should waste, nor is a sheet of paper, a threadbare doll or a pair of socks—nor an opportunity to slap a coat of empathy onto just about anything.

Born on August 11, 1932, the fourth of five girls, Phoebe (Smale) Marrall grew up in the dusty town of El Cajon, California. Theirs was the family you might find written into a film script if you wanted to portray the impoverished, the backward, the extremely emotionally wounded. In an unfinished memoir, she describes herself and her sisters as "feral, ashamed, fearful, intelligent, unsocialized, and deprived of comforts and sustenance." The phrase *damaged goods* certainly applies. Except for the Disney films *Snow White and the Seven Dwarves* and *Pinocchio*, the world of entertainment was denied the five Smale girls. They dressed in hand-me-downs. To call his children in for supper, the girls' father, an undiagnosed paranoid schizophrenic, would shoot at them with a BB gun and giggle at the way they'd run for dear life. And during that meal, no talking was allowed. The dinner table was not a place for family socializing. "The daughters were cogs on the parental gear. Protest was punishable."

In the same incomplete memoir, Phoebe recalls her mother's death in 1941: "One of her symptoms was an inability to keep her eyes sufficiently open. A fatigue of some sort also ravaged her. She couldn't handle the housework and finally around the week before Christmas, she took to her bed. The two youngest daughters never saw her again; the three oldest had to help transfer her to the 'good' bedroom.... What funeral services had been arranged were disallowed for the daughters."

Of her father's death just two months after her mother's, this has been recorded in the same body of work: "He took to lying down on the dining room cot. He worsened. Someone decided each of the girls would spend one day a week staying home from school to care for him. No one explained how each girl was to do this. When it was my turn I took to my heels at the goat barn, not once checking on our father. Who knew if he needed a glass of water? Who knew if he needed assistance rising from the cot? Still feeling ill, he donned the only suit and tie he had and drove to a neighbor's home. Could the neighbor drive him to San Diego to the Naval Hospital? The neighbor did assist him. The death certificate indicates he was admitted at four o'clock p.m. on February 24, 1942. He died at four o'clock the following morning. None of this was known until the children's grandmother told them when they arrived home from school: 'your papa is gone.'" Accordingly, two of the sisters remembered joining hands and dancing in joy: their father couldn't hurt them anymore.

Phoebe was an orphan at the age of nine.

As an adult, she saw a therapist four days a week for thirty-five years.

* * *

"I have been writing daily, as usual, but something is in the way," Marrall wrote, in March of 1998; and in November of that same year: "Too many chores and tasks come down when all I want to do is take long, uninterrupted hours and work at delicious words and phrases… I get pulled into my subjects and find my work changes character. That is a problem… I can't think I'll EVER have to worry about having nothing to do, as much as I love my labor."

In January of 2000, to an imaginary editor, she described her labor: "The impulse for poetry, as you of all people know, is different from the craft. The impulse for, or of, poetic imagery, or of the moment ephemeral comes in the Great Silence for me. Thus: I wish to put morning streets in darkness and desertedness into a, or several, poem(s), but I can't. My maturity, my poetic majority, has not been reached. I am not there yet. I haven't put the harness together for wearing on the lead of poetry."

Readers of *Relief, Have You A Name?* will likely disagree. Marrall has indeed succeeded in reaching poetic ripeness. She retrieved from the mind's sky of thoughts that which might be termed abstract, pinned it down, and formed it into tangible phrases for the readers' delight and rumination. In imagery like:

I shall work away at partials,
excising the winged pests of
duty and necessity

from "A Modest Proposal" and:

> *Could I learn to be friends*
> *with a mile laid end to end*
> *with all the others, and thank it?*

from "Into the Days of Hours," the reader finds clean reference to the poet's allegiance to humility and to contemplation. "The Enigma of Impending Doom" exposes the poet's tender layer of angst, like continually healing skin, residing just below the surface of her own vulnerability and speculation:

> *News, dire and various,*
> *stalks me like subtle enemies.*
> *Relief, have you a name?*
> *Is your velvet a weave*
> *softened by wear?*
>
> *I find no softnesses,*
> *no cushioning silks;*
> *nesting is barbarous.*
> *I am pinned, the bark and knots*
> *of logs holding me straitened.*

The student of Phoebe Marrall's poetry is invited to consider things anew. In "A Film of Morning Lingers," she alludes to the notion of expanding one's awareness:

> *This veiled light*
> *has a half-life*
> *of one second.*
> *No beacon, or flare,*
> *or spilled flame can seduce*
> *a soul for whom understatement*
> *is so short-lived.*
> *A film of morning lingers*
> *across the lavender window:*
> *pure invitation to partake*
> *in a slow gaze for all reverie*
> *is worth. Pity the unseeing*

who do not search
for the seductress
of early morning.

Why not, she suggests, give in to smelling the roses now and again?

Marrall is certainly not above existential self-effacement, baring it all in "Don't Worry, Little Poem":

I won't write you and team us up in despair.
No iron shoes, no taut lines for you.
I, strafed and straitened, bow in the harness,
I shall let you go free.
No, you needn't accompany me.
Your beauty stands without me.
You, flinging an un-arrestable glance,
must not be bruised by the impatience
and haste of your pretentious mistress.

The enthralled reader will encounter in Phoebe Marrall's poetry the ordinary made beautiful. A seventy-five-watt bulb is revered; a pink bar of soap becomes a tiny spider's tombstone. Chores are recipients of the poet's wrath—and why not? They wedge themselves between the writer and her muses. Never mind that they occasionally *are* the muses. Partaking of Marrall's poetry is a bit like having a ringside seat to the human psyche, in her case complete with acrobats of insight, untamed curiosity, her chosen words clothed in alluring, light-catching finery.

* * *

While much of her art was displayed on the walls of her home, and therefore viewed by all who came to visit, the same cannot be said of her poetry. It was closeted, so to speak, and remained unpublished during her lifetime. She died on February 1, 2017.

Phoebe Marrall had two daughters, Jane and Camille, from her first brief marriage. It is their intention that their mother's legacy be remembered with as much grace, wit, honesty, intelligence, and grit as the poems in this collection testify. Chances are, she would want it dedicated to Jerry Marrall. For thirty-one years he was the love of her life. She once said that he was the finest, kindest, most thoughtful man she had ever met. Her daughters also loved him and considered him to be their father.

—*Gayle Jansen Beede*

part one

I search with my eyes
against the small distribution of time I have.
Poetry doesn't have to have a message.
Painting doesn't have to be illustration.

Mortality is a thin gouache
which laves over and through our pores,
and dries in powder-brush,
like faint silt under our eyes.
Wind-carried, it settles so lightly
we do not feel it until we fall
in its gale of dust.

LEGACY

We came from scraps,
pulling slowly away from wrath
of spiderwebs and manure powder
and the reek of claret.

"Destitute" we brought with us,
in the remembered glossy wool fiber
of the hand-me-down sweater,
and old, brown coat of no warmth.

Someone had noted, "…five small
children left destitute." This word
was new to us. Having nothing
now had a name. It erased images

of old geranium stems,
and an open can of extra milk,
well blackened with flies,
in the barn, by the stanchion.

It did not include the spread of pink
pepper-berries, the tiny ring
found hanging on a weathered spear of
goat-yard fence, the darting barn swallow.

It declared a possession-lessness and
a mine without ore for milling
into middle class blend. It said there
was no money, or socks, or toys.

But in truth we brought much
with us, as we could not
shed the clothes we wore or the
fear, or the certainty of dire eyes.

We brought the scraps and spiderwebs
and the deep red ring of dried

wine at the bottom of a glass left
long by the radio, familiar, sour.

"Destitute," as now we have blouses
hanging on metal hangers, and shoes
never approved of by our father?
"Destitute" in dry, warm houses?

Having nothing in our letter-day
provision, the use of money?
Is there not a partial wealth in hot,
running water, and a righteous sink?

We have our bodies' warmth against
cold, and fear of administered pain,
and the wrack of fury in precision.
There is possession in free time.

Yes, there is destitution in our veins.
As much as we have quit the dark
and left El Cajon to desiccate in
the wind, it sticks like windblown burrs.

SURRENDER

There is labor in all of it.
Grainy minutes, pinpricks of sun,
wayward bugs and words
passing slowly. I hunch for breath.

Can I not *do* something? Escape?
Brush away aphids, walk faster
before the dusk of memories
overtakes me? Such mortal weariness

in waiting, such exhaustion.
And no place to stop.
There are shades and light,
and wind outdoors, but no relief.

If wind could clothe, my wraps
would always be clean. But this
is rude country, edged like frost
on leaves. Edged, dark and charred—

the devil licks its blade. Surrender
is a sea of rude, surly foam
where crude words crash
like hurled bricks. We were girls

without girlhood, where wonder
calcified into uncertainty, born
from a mother so surrendered
her very shadow disappeared.

IN THE GLOW OF HAVING BEEN OBSCURE

We were the good children of 1944.

In those classroom days we
were mostly smart, and sat
in desks secured in lines.

Then some of us went away
and settled like dust in
different classrooms, eager
to be liked, high and mighty.

Now that we're separated,
our indentured memories revisit
old classmates' faces, names—
the high-top shoes of the boy scribbling
at the chalkboard, trousers puckering
at his lean waist. Valleys of grass
from earlier sown seed
divide us from each other now:
disunited, working, some killed in war.

And while we were still pushing
and scrambling for equilibrium,
unseen by our peers of 1944,
printer's ink appeared on obituary columns.

NOT LITTLE GIRLS

It was the year of Kate Smith
singing broadly, a big world
wrapped around a little world,
which would eclipse it in the end.
The War came, ungrasped
by us children, me at least.
Likewise came convoys
wheeling past like bugs
with legs drawn up inside—
soldiers inside the open-ended trucks
leaning forward from side benches,
waving at us, me at least, in a manner
of grown up men, big Army men.
We took them all to be acting
as if we were older, like young women,
not little girls, waving not as fathers
or as big brothers, but as if they were
flirting with us. Someone said
they were going to the "ears"
on the distant hill, to listen for the Japs,
which is what we called them,
not yet knowing the difference
between insult and respect.

THE HOUSE

In wan sunlight, silent,
chalked and vined, the house simply was.
Like an old woman it bore itself
into the morning: fidgeting with pigeons
on its roofs, and winking at
the light with a pane broken through
by some old broom handle or
a baseball missiled by a child
misbehaving in the first lot nearby
before it was blackened over
for the stabling of bull cars.

The house was slow in waking up,
even when a fusty Pomeranian scurried from
the front door on a leash,
held by a woman who clopped down
cement steps in bright blue slippers.

From a distance, the house ruminated on
the beetling black and green cars
parked along the curb of the sanitary
office building next door.
It warmed and faintly quickened,
and breathed out redolence of old upholstery,
bath soap, cleaning powder, overripe fruit in a bowl.
It was heaped like some supine, gestating
animal, slow moving, with low metabolism,
in the morning, to be roused only partially
by the winds of workaday currents.

What it appeared to be was up for transformation.
Boards, paint, plumbing, leaded glass, a light switch.
Weltering upon weltering of lath and plaster
entirely obliterated by the wreck's blast.
The nobility of the ancient being, raped in broad daylight,
was prismed into certainty by the flash of a scattering
light force. Destroyed, the flesh and bones of the house lived.

SECRET COALS

for my therapist

There was no comforting,
or warming, when he went away.
The leave-taking was short.
It narrowed further as the door closed.

The sessions rubbed. Reddened and
exhausted, my eyes closed over
what absence was left me. My mouth
could not swallow its powdered dryness.
His eyes seemed to survey
nothing. He dared not blink.

From dry hours of afternoon visits
no conflagration, no secret coals.
A brittle cracking and snap,
and he was gone.

IN ISOLATION

Where shall I spend today?
In the cocoa stuccoed house,
bold along my homeward way.
In pinkened walls I shall play.

I enter into rooms of clay
alongside spider, bug and mouse,
and I see dancers, flutists—stay,
with me, circle, chant and pray.

Bare feet, sandals, black and gray,
halt for ceremonial carouse,
then step again in noise, display,
and we are part of this array.

Tomorrow I shall spend my day
in empty rooms of an empty house.
White with black, its silence may
hold for me my yesterday.

SOMEWHERE IN THE DILUVIA OF TRIADS

Yesterday I tried to write a poem
about the seedpods that clatter down
over everything in summer's ripeness.
They're impossible to clean up.

It isn't the way they clutter,
it isn't the way I must sweep and sweep.
It isn't that their orange does not stain.
It is my reaction to them.

How do I develop form?
What are the length and breadth of it?
Its economy, aesthetic?

The form I want to construct has its frame,
I suppose, in the battle of the tree
and me: I know the orange rain
and cannot protect against it.

Who wants a shower of mess
where cars and trash cans
have their places, and people crunch
by on the sidewalk?

Somewhere in the diluvia of triads
and perfect calyces is impertinence,
and recurrent energy popping down anew.
How can they be so endless?

A BOAT IN AN EDDY

In this midday pool, shallow, quiet,
I sit with the water lapping
at my waist. It is warm, it is cold,
like divided winds.
To come to the shores of this water
we started out much earlier.

The pool has lazed here,
but the path to it is crooked,
quite crooked.
The walking stick must be planted,
and leaned upon
so the path will stay in place.
It cannot be walked like a sidewalk.

I am in turns and S's, like
a boat in an eddy.
In danger of losing footing I slow,
not knowing if the path will straighten.
I journey to this pool, losing
my bearings as the trail loses its straight.

A MODEST PROPOSAL

Today I shall make a small list,
a 15-minute intervals list of things to do,
and avoid time-consuming projects.

My list will be adaptable and more
or less random, but purposeful.
It will bind mop to primrose.

I intend to Get Things Done
bit by bit by bit, which, together
will prove me industrious and persevering.

I shall work away at partials, excising
the winged pests of duty and necessity.
Out of mind, someday yes…

I won't have wasted my life.

SUN ORANGE

As little morning suns,
as beaming open mouths
in a water-filled saucer,
as flowers in thin rinds,
discarded orange cups
sit in formation.
I drink up my juice.
The orange cups beam
open-mouthed, calling
to mind my hunger.

MY MOON, MY FULL MOON

I possess her like a pearl
because she is there for the taking.
Or is it that she possesses me?
Like a moth, I flutter and creep
in her 5:00 a.m. light, dancing
in the shadow of trees,
clothing myself in
the yellow and silver
she furnishes so freely.

MY WALLET OF AGING

Can't I still reach for that lace?
I've hardly begun to smooth it over my hips.
In theory, I should be able to *think young*—
upscale chocolates, profiteroles,
a trip to Victoria's Secret,
cocktails at noon—but in the company
of youth, I've stepped on the fragile cover
and fallen through. Shelves of fragrance,
outrageous shoes, that shiny gold chain,
are cordoned off. I've lost a little fear,
true, and carry a little money now.
But it can't be blown on a liberal spill
of "Walnut Rose." I also carry
a burden of fear.

AWAY FROM SPEEDING LAUGHTER

Away, out of sight, beyond strong leaves,
I want enclosure, and bonds of soft wool
to cradle myself away from speeding laughter,
and the noise pushing up-down, up-down when,
barely seated, I am carried off to the side.

So *this* is a surfer wedding, I say to the person
next to me, who happens to be me in ennui.
These young heads are crowned with perfect sun-spray;
I have noticed them tossed, and stilled when the
bridal couple edges toward them in flip-flops and boots.

This is affluent casual, so cool it moves words from
out of the mouths of babes to the breath of old folks,
and pulls me by the ear to the mic of the wedding docent.
She emcees us into Hawaiian rock-and-roll, and the baited
back-and-forth of guys and girls who dance with abandon.

No, my white wool does not enclose or cradle me away
from the pitch of custom and rolling decibel.
It spreads itself as thin as smoke and whitens all.

THE PINK BAR OF SOAP

I am seized by impulse
to flurrying words
and their meanings out of control
to finally speak cleverly
of finding the corpse.

These insulting ideas
mount; I parry and scuttle
them like dried leaves,
themselves more apt,
not clever, not handy.

A sprawling spider,
so tiny it's no wonder
its grave embraced it, generously
and conveniently, unnoticed by
whoever washed his hands.

It trod the cantilevered
bar in fragile, sure stepping;
a giant's hand took the soap,
clasped it with the other,
and killed its infancy.

The giant didn't look, the
babe didn't see to escape
its instant demise, but met
death, preserved as a lovely
star for me to wish upon.

VACANCY

I was in the dining room
to vacuum up bugs.
I hated to do it,
but them beasties are thugs.

I sucked up ants
and cockroach egg cases,
and maybe a termite
tying its shoelaces.

I thought to empty
when I was done,
the bag and the beasties
but there were none!

I had swallowed up
webs and ants,
but I seemed to have lost
my search and destroy track.

In the future in my house
watch where you walk,
and listen closely.
Them beasties might talk.

75-WATT BULB

The jewel box, this cube of light
set small and brilliant among
ash-dark boxes on the roof,
shows me through all this
dusty, never-ending night
the attic window's lone bulb.

CATALYST OF BOBBY PINS

From this backward look
at my white teenage years, to how
it was, I look now at how it is,
and hope I have risen above
adolescence. But have I really?

In how it was, we are laughing
and primping white girls pulling
bobby pins out of our hair before
the eight o'clock bell and have no
notion of others except ourselves.

Still, I cannot forget the weary
black woman washing a toilet
in one of the stalls, wordless,
seemingly resigned to cleaning white
girls' lavatories, to having this kind of job.

THE FRAGILE

Like cattle in the stock hauler's truck,
we stand captured, our minds rigidly in place.
We ride in the hiatus between beginning and end.
Loaded aboard and forced to stay
in position for transfer allows no flexure or relief.

Where have small rhythms dissipated?
Where and when and why have circling visions gone?
We are straitened on all sides, stacked three high.
Presumed insensate, we are imprisoned
too close to the hooves and horns of others.

AWAITING DIAGNOSIS

Thunder and smoke
have broken and dried my days.

There was mutual exclusivity
until pain enveloped us.

It was not my pain but his
at midnight.

Like rocks in a stream
tests and questions came.

Morphine, IV, sleep
afforded surcease.

What is it, what will they find
when more is observed?

A cherry stone, a diverticular
cache, a bubble?

They will look, search gently
and tell us *something*.

I will redouble my trying
to comfort and learn.

THE RIGHT SUPPLIES

"Yes. I shall do it," I sigh.
Thus begins my medical training.

Enough to last a week, the right supplies
grow on the sink board.

I've purchased gauzes and saline.
Paper tape is new to me.

Polysporin and Silvadine become
staples in tubes and jars. You see,

my husband's skull is growing cancer.
What do I know about squamous cells?

Buried woven material and sutures
are now commonplace at the wound site.

Nightly, my chair-side work is done.
The patient adjusts himself

in his chair. I learn to bring supplies
on a tray. I should be less heavy-handed;

I'm no Clara Barton or Dorothea Dix.
This sweet, gentle man coaches by

mapping out his pain for me.

part two

In the wealth of pens and pencils
I have found and collected while running in grassy fields
or descending hospital basement steps
or stopping at the ATM where some soul
has forgotten his ballpoint cum advertising novelty,
I have the experience of windfall luxury.
The gravel-bitten pen I brought to life still writes:
what was rare once and now is common remains rare to me.
A real pencil, a real pen…

I look for money, successfully, and scavenge art-ready objects,
perhaps, I rationalize, not missed by anyone.
Homeless coins speak to me from the running track;
a digital watch lies by the drinking fountain
on the football turf.
The random discovery, the unexpected fortune—
I need extra fingers to hold it all.

THE DAYS WERE GETTING SHORTER

For days, when the afternoon sun
was thin as broth, and the bare, sage twigs
blackened against the rocks,
they let the dog out to get his run.
They remarked again
that the days were getting shorter.
If they could have seen themselves,
they would have recognized soft stones,
worn by habit into forms
that might have settled
into an oil painting.

LOVELY EMPTINESS

The black glass doors hold promise
as much as the gold of sunlight
welcomes entry into afternoon's
still empty, propitious setting.

Such stark and lovely emptiness
absorbs me, my lovely, wandering
illumination, my hearty attention
redolent with the Cantata No. 51.

Glass before black emptiness
is engraved with what-is-in-there?
holding pulse and object, wonderment
and unpreparedness palpable.

A FILM OF MORNING LINGERS

This veiled light
has a half-life
of one second.
No beacon, or flare,
or spilled flame can seduce
a soul for whom understatement
is so short-lived.
A film of morning lingers
across the lavender window:
pure invitation to partake
in a slow gaze for all reverie
is worth. Pity the unseeing
who do not search
for the seductress
of early morning.

THE ECHO I NEEDED TO COMFORT

More than once I planned
a lovely morning.
The gray and all-invited
foraging by foot among
old leaves, dry, brittle,
for the noise I needed,
the echo I needed to comfort
my un-cushioned ear
assaulted by silence.

More than once I entered
such a lovely morning.
It always returned
unheard breakage of an
old leaf, bowed, arched,
with a yield of a season's
resonance just waiting for
a chance to let loose its clamor
and bang and crash.

THE SCARS THEREOF

Is there more poured into
being a mother than a
mother can hold?
The baby comes, "It's
a girl," they say, and a
breath of relief hushes
the exuberance of
nurses around the
obstetrician who holds
the child upside down
and gives the world to it.

Birth, the original violence
offering indignation at our
introduction to the world,
cannot help itself or the
baby, or the mother whose
labors now begin for time
extended into oblivion,
or the wars, or the scars
thereof, or discordant music
percussive and unrhythmic,
without ritardando.

I RISE IN A MORNING UNTOUCHED

Out of memories of my father, May 1996

An avenue of words,
soot-filled mornings,
dire nights,
afternoons of
      length and sun,
his profanity.

Disordering anger, measured thunder,
loss of power. Stone and pebble,
threaded needle,
twice thrown ropes, the word strings
trailed through, trailed after
the impulse of wrath.

These words were not
for utterance by us children.
They came wrapped in fire.
Unwrapping would burn.
Such might belonged only to the
      mighty.
He was the only one allowed
      combustion.

NOTES FOR A POEM

So fragile she is,
white as eggshell.
Almost visible, pushed by wind.
Once, her eyes held treasures, stars,
and a night-blossom, and grass for goats.
But the blindness that affected me once
affects her now.

I try to catch too much.
Confusion has over-swept her for these long decades.
Before that current there was explosion,
fire, falling timbers, hail of ashes,
burning vitriol, blazing lava
too violent, application of death,
soul of no life, demon in hate.
The reed with eyes of deep crescents
suffered bruise and brace.
She stands in a lifetime of effort.
Even my view of her is violent
and stands to damage her.
My opinions are wooden blocks,
my remarking breath burns her.
The bruise cannot be hid.

THIS CURIOSITY

Patience had asked me to
wait out a promise. I tried,
suffering impulse to uproot.
A rosette was growing.

Flowering, no
outward sign of growth
but a healthy green spread.
I waited and kept alive this curiosity.

A year, itself gestating from fall to
fall to spring, treasured on with a
spiral flattened in broad leaves,
and holes eaten through by larvae.

Then, spring, that segment of season
proffering riches and surge,
brought up the rosette into branching
stems bearing calyces and promise.

This rosette let loose all its inner
thunder, and pulsed out with long
arms of leaves, then buds
and yellow flowers in the night.

This narrative deserves revision
to be equal to the transformation
of the rosette. Re-write about this
now six-foot juggernaut awaits.

Yellow flowers of four-lobed petals,
freshness from night to early morning,
fade and droop in the terrible sun, and
my books have found it out.

Hooker's Primrose.

PICK OUT A CLOUD

He said, "Pick out a cloud…"
He held the weighted spear
and suggested quite loud
the trajectory was clear.

I held the other lance,
its grip drawing my fist.
I copied his experienced stance
aimed too in skyward clasping.

Away and ho! I flung my piece.
Sure in plant, thrower's toss.
A riffling cloud, a wispy fleece
hung lovely white, in kapok floss.

The arc and rod twinned for flight.
They took their leave in breathy rush,
in some control, and purposed might
against still air, in sound and in hush.

I stepped along in closely fit measure.
The distance of my javelin throw
among Coke cans, grassy treasures,
was sunk in muddy clover-grow.

New Balance prints laid fifty-nine.
His throw swept over twice and more
the distance roughly-measured mine,
to generate a private roar.

The javelin is indeed warlike.
But in beauty takes the air,
its rimless climb ascending hike,
through draft and zephyr, on skyward stair.

PICK OUT A CLOUD II

"Pick out a cloud," he said.
Aim higher than the leaves
brushing against the forehead of the wind.

Set yourself a long aim
like a spider's leg flung
in capture.

Poise yourself, spring-loaded
for uncoiled departure
of this lance, lately a part of you.

Watch the spinning silver
pierce and ride the zephyr
until it overtakes that gentleness.

Watch steadily its fall
in strong, unwayward arc
to green receiving grass and mudded roots.

Hear, like a distant echo
your own yell in expense
of energy thrown to sky, to cloud.

The javelin, guided
by your hand, now guides your
eyes, following, irresistibly drawn.

WHERE I HAVE MY LANDMARKS

I was in the housing of black dawn.
The night images in their quiet
had monitored what I had not,
and yielded them up to me.

Strange deservedness had its sentries:
for whom did those traffic lights post
their rhythmic green, yellow and red
in intersections hollow and empty?

I came through as a rude,
aggressive driver, pedaling from gas to brake,
unnoticed by lurking roofs
or dewy poles beaming alternating lights.

They stood, I passed, in the black,
yawning faintly gray, faintly loosening.
I crossed the night/dawn meridian,
listening in on the change of hours.

Tomorrow, I shall invade the dawn
again, pressing the accelerator and going
where I've planted my landmarks...lumps of
houses against the sky, and a solid green light.

DASEIN

There isn't room, I shout.
Take these spider-legged smoke whorls
and uncurl them, their gray
        to pale, like white dyed cotton.
Such smudge and dust must not embed.

Am I kin to morning's lives?
How is it, with my blood, and
        morning's pulse,
and cardiac excitements? I
cannot capture much,
even if my breath is a net cast into the air.

A furtive light casts a weak dawn
inside that house, pale morning tea,
        wan, thin,
without real glow. I saw it,
hoped it into heating
my wrought iron so sturdy with cold.

INTO THE DAYS OF HOURS

There are no small miles.
Into the days of hours we rode,
through the Sand Hills, over
bridges, over denuded pavement.

When we crashed through
the speed limit, hurtling
onward and onward,
the mile remained 5,280 feet.

Could I learn to be friends
with a mile laid end to end
with all the others, and thank it?
Did it not deliver us safely?

All in the mile, my breaths
came sharply, our wheels
obeyed our pilot, impatience
grew, I tried to fall asleep.

The chore of riding with others
could be measured
by the mile and minute.
I wanted to leap from the car.

Now, the miles are behind us.
We are at rest from speed.
What curtailment of violent impulse
I learned I shall exercise.

THE ENIGMA OF IMPENDING DOOM

A circle of sharpened
upright logs engirdles me.
These unyielding poles
enclose me, unbidden, in
sudden woeful quantity.

News, dire and various,
stalks me like subtle enemies.
Relief, have you a name?
Is your velvet a weave
softened by wear?

I find no softnesses,
no cushioning silks;
nesting is barbarous.
I am pinned, the bark and knots
of logs holding me straitened.

No resistance is possible.
I stand supported by the
closeness of bad news.
Relief, do you lie flung,
splintered, fallen to quiescence?

DO YOU WANT A POEM?

Possibility opposes
my small defiance
and takes root in
my slumber.
Yes, I cried in small cries,
I want to do,
I want to calm
what thrashes.
But stillness has no pool
or settling pond.
I gesture and am not soothed.

Should a pot of pearl paint
be shaken before the cap is undone?

Should sedimentary frost follow
thick flow or undisturbed lavender
and glaze by accident?

Imprisoned and roiling
like unsettled gold, I plunge
emulsive light, never increasing.

WHAT IS VIRTUE TO ONE IS CARDINAL SIN TO THE OTHER

I speak from two mouths, using
the words of one against the other.
This is not a debate; it is strophe and antistrophe.
And yet, more than this.
It is fulcrumic. It is premise and proof.

What is virtue to one
is cardinal sin to the other.
(My mouths adopt articulations
not their own, for the sake of example;
one magnifies the other.)

Husband/wife are "one" says one voice,
so certain. It has been indoctrinated.
"Two shall become one," say priests and
protestants, and no one asks, "One what?"
In voice, the idea forms and hardens,
like epoxy left to dry the bonding.
It secures the disparate two.

The formation has been conceived,
in error. Bone and bone rarely meet.
Contraction turns the lipped joint downward.
The yoke holds; insistent voices strain
against wooden caution.
No matter the enlarged or shrunken shoulders,
the yoke must hold.
A second voice cries in agony of another
marriage, trying to die.
The South pulls at its Mason-Dixon line,
determined to undo straps and leathered minds.
The Union, the states, the free, the enslaved,
The Nation according to the North,
secession according to the South.

The marriage according to the North!

Separation according to the South!
"One must be two or die!"
"Two must be one or die!"
Honesty got farther than "Two shall be one,"
ipso facto, by decree, "I thus pronounce,"
and nearly broke the epoxy permanence.

According to where your choir loft seats you,
you sing north or south, sometimes in harmony.
Sometimes you sing with a mouth inflamed
but unheard until its stridency comes, discordant,
and your antistrophe cannot wait
and they clap their hands over their ears.

AUDEN USED A LAUNDRY LIST

Relief from responsibility:
devoutly wished.
The infusion of satisfaction
in accomplishment:
devoutly welcomed.

My paper thoughts can be folded up
and pocketed. I prefer vellum to tissue.

Surcease, lovely interval, calm after outraged storming,
air aplenty after densities of steam, small recesses shielded
from torrent, silence after thunder. I have come to marvel at you.
Thank you for turning your relief toward me.

Freud used discards.
Auden used a laundry list.
Rodia imbedded shards.
I use intangibles as best I can.

part three

Why should delight and amazement make me drop silent,
and why does intensity paralyze me?

*

Before I die I want to have survived a few more narrow escapes
from insignificance…
I am afraid death will come to me when I am not looking,
in such an airless circumstance.
Collage can supply vapidity, with no color much to speak of.
I can work with scraps and fixative, and as I once said in a poem,
I will leave my print with unjustified permanence.
Will capturing insignificance and living through it give me conquest over
lack?

THE VERY THINGS POETIZED

There are times when poetry
turns me off, with its predictable
lines, sentiment, artifice.

I am embarrassed by simple,
discrete images laid out
in personal lento.

As I have lingered over
the very things poetized,
I wish another not to.

MY apple, MY bent nail,
MY basketry must not be
duplicated as cipher.

As I study stanza and verse
I fear I can
merely imitate beauty.

SONNET AFTER LUNCH

Afloat on waves of parqueted bricks
a sail with green boughed masts;
I played and wheeled the noonday mix
alongside birds scavenging the wake in blasts.

Twit and sit, their legs go,
black and shiny, strutting posts
tripods curled, flag-wing furled
nip the air with preening beak.

Beak and claw, no slightest flaw
Breaks zip/zip hop to my thrown crumb
A duck and quickstep
A flick and backstep
A small and wary tight-quilled drum.

Hello, bird
With monocular vision
Had yet met me more
Ye'd know my. . .

I love your black and yellow ringed eye
Your startling dips and bobbing neck
Your hollow bone, gray tone
Your set up, sit up, tweezer peck.

PERFECTING

Whom should I listen to?
In the shallows of memo-writing,
leather scraps and cord,
the punch and glue can;
I am stuck with perfecting.
"...a good job, well done."

Imbued and unfiltered, run through
with dissatisfaction, embalmed
with criticism from voices now echoing
with what they let fall: sharp-chipped,
I stir, and watch the dust in sunlight
and listen to the deejay buried in his plastic
                housing.

I'D NEVER TITLE A POEM "HOPE"

Find a thought, little heart.
Beat, beat, find a way out.
Search and seek, look
straight into the light.
Look in dark, too, look more.

My heart, my eyes, still search.
Recesses contain ore.
My finger feels along, pokes.
My heart supposes relief
where there is only night.

HOLLOWS AND POCKETS

Often, I'd wandered
ragged-ankled and sandy,
in that soft-blown dim atmosphere
of corrosive imagination,
in gray stroked light.

Falling, my mind filled
hollows and pockets
like interminable rain.
I caught drops and streams
in overflowing cups
green, white, gold
and drenched my flight.

FLEEING

We'll be going again across the sage desert.
The sun will be blue as it slants
across morning hills mute, and distant, and still.

We will see those same new skies
and pinion pines and cut banks.
Oh yes, we'll remember, there is
that line of trees along the crest
that made me think of accessibility before.

Thoughts that came to me where the highway
put the naked, vast slope into view
will be melancholy again, unanchored.
We will be going seventy, eighty, past the
rotating, barren, deserted mountain.

We will be fleeing along those
virgin miles again, dropping foolish
and working Los Angeles out the window.

The license plates will read "California"
on the speeding capsule cars with
young drivers soloing past, gleamingly.
They can't be bothered to ease up
and let Salt Lake City come when it will.

GLIMPSE AND SATURATION

This morning at the farmers' market
again, ephemera.
I wander in the un-rushing, along plywood tables
holding root and greens, and pale Asian pears.
Without sun yet, tomatoes shine nevertheless,
swollen to readiness, so pregnant.

Purpose, and money, and supper planning dissolve.
Here is a thin silk blouse over a T-shirt
on a small woman chatting in Vietnamese.
Fashion ingenuous: tiny beads in a burst of
embroidery cluster at the neckline of a black
blouse; the lady's skirt is printed Hawaiian cotton.

Buckles, a woven gold filament, leather braided
across naked toes, a counter broken under, cradling
a bony heel, and Reeboks reeking of white
are priced at One Poem Per Each.
I delight in the nonsense!

On one table, at its right edge,
there is garlic laid in an unbound pile.
Each bulb has had its roots carefully pared away
so the bottom shows a bare white disc, a seal,
a moon, delicate papery light.
The moon upon moon upon moon—I must leave, or I cannot.

GO, AND FEAST YOUR EYES

You must go down and visit those dream sites:
black places in hot parking lots, corners in
asphalt nearly melted, shimmering with white lines
and absolutely still in lethargic midday sun.

You must go to those forests Made in China:
lamps in boxes and fake flowers spilling from racks
mounted high above your reach with perfumed candles
and plastic Halloween pumpkins on rods.

You should go to the stark yardage rolls:
scrim cloth and light linen evened out above damask
and upholstery covering woven maroon and white,
and common broadcloth in starry prints.

The dream-fields, empty as they are fixed:
they await habitation, as dried mud awaits water,
for new fingering of red and blue plastic tote bags
and catchment of your eye in the solitude of pleasure.

THE SAME PRIVACY

These I saw: small onions laid
with their root discs punctuating
the longitude poles. Polar caps,
yes, navels to the earth where
their buried unions still hold.

That space along the stalls,
unpeopled on this damp morning,
stops me (for it insists), with the
white parking lines leaping
to the distant edge of gray asphalt,
and to the gray and black
of my mind's caverns.
There is beauty and there is
the comfort of isolation,
desolation remembered.
Why (I ask myself)
should I crave *this* comfort,
which would seem black, dead?

I walk in this same privacy
where the dead black
chicken house vibrates in the stink
of manure, and winds from the west,
and the dead black of a remembered
gas tank rising by the road?
Does the pensive void pull me
to the empty, and therefore personal,
paving, begetting a sage
from my wilderness to give life
to the vacancy?

OUT FROM THE EPICENTER

A turbulence of earthquakes
has etched rivers through
my stucco plains.

Its engravings thread,
lightning forms, from the
epicenter out into vastness.

Not until some determined
handyman caulks them white
will they dry up.

And where they disappear
will flow other rivers,
long in new courses.

The daddy longlegs and
trestle builders will direct them,
and replenish my plains.

BASINS OF SOUND

There is no top. There are always further heights to reach.
—Jascha Heifetz, Lithuanian-born violinist

Once in a while,
the drifts of what I hear
arc above muddy sounds,
and their permanence is sensible,
I am glad to sharpen my listening.

Will I, like the young who need
high volume sound piped into their
ears until the throbs beat again,
attune my listening only to my whims?

My ears, catchment basins of sound
and filters against the cacophony
which is merely noise, increase keenly,
and reach beyond the familiar,
and learn anew as Heifetz did.

THE PSYCHE IN WAITING

Teal blue the naugahyde,
pale green the dividers,
a row house of chairs stood anchored.

Prompt and well-oiled, the elevator
opened and closed, closed and opened.
The floor bore quiet foot traffic.

Restless the psyche in waiting,
witness the unending watcher.
People went down and up and down.

For the languishing, rest in sitting,
for the chatterer, audience.
The stressed simply slept.

The hospital picks petals
from the blossom patients
and sets them upright for attention.

A PAEAN TO BEING HOME

The catch-cornered room
reserved for me
emptied its vacancy
for my possession.

I brought in all the boulders
and dog smells, books
unpeeled, and parking places
collected in distant hours.

But I left motion and motor outside.
My room had no space for the violence
of traveling, high speed, fear of eighteen-
wheelers spinning at eighty.

For my ease, the reserved room
breathed quiet, and absence of
forced invasion up the interstate,
and noise of the passing gears.

I let the quiet and its particular
liveliness tickle over me
like leaves of aspen blowing
green and silver in the sun.

My quiet, enlarging room
has its own noon and night,
its hours resplendent in
active gold, catching light.

RED

I must cut those red berries.
I must cut the sprays long
outside my window, silent
pop beads, nodding proffers
of fecundity and ripening.

In twenty-five years, I have
not seen berries on this bush,
or more than tiny brown
knobs dried on lengths of stems
unproductive of fruit and color.

I shall lay the freshly cut berries
on pretty paper, and center them
on the oak table which draws the
sunlit morning through another
window, and have myself some red.

THE GRAY SPIDER

Without announcement
or effort at display
or notice of me except
as I make shadow and motion,
a spider hangs below the soap bar.

She, or he, cradles the air
with legs pencil-line thin,
and waves one to search past
its own cradling and fragility,
knowing empty space very well.

I, we, whole parts of me,
seeing palest gray before enamel white,
refrain from immediate transferring;
I only speak in invitation.
Would you like to hang elsewhere?

It answers very clearly, so I
sickle across invisibility with
an orange pencil: a trapeze made
for gentling a spider's rope over
to a new landing place.

Those unsteady legs, the gray bulb
of its body now right side up,
a sense that guides scrambling,
equips the air-cradler to escape
and leave an empty crescent in my air.

SAID TO A DROWNED DADDY LONGLEGS

Oh.   Oh.   Oh.
I thought you were a wisp of grass
brought into the shower on my feet.
Yet, I wondered, for you looked
like summer grass, brown and dry.
In March, no grass is dried and dead.
To see what you actually were,
I peered long and close, as I should've
before causing closeted rain.
I would have shut off the nozzle!
Your parachute-string legs could have
climbed the air to safety. Instead,
they lie in wilted length,
roots from your drowned body,
orderly, thin, whole.
I leave you to dry in death,
in return to pre-genital quiescence.

GIVE ME NO WAN LIGHT

Distant, weak, uncourageous,
un-warm shadow spread grayly,
that so-called light barely alive
is blinking out. Not a candle flame,
nor fodder from any muse, it
possesses no attachments,
burning in flimsy constancy,
mirroring elan vital.

FALLING LEAVES OF WHITE PAPER

"We'd like to talk with you."
So I went to the school's office
and saw a folder open like a bible
in the counselor's hand.
"Look at these," they said.
Squinting, I looked at
falling leaves of white paper.

I was seeing corpses of my writing:
skewed shadows, words
written in my hand but
not by me. How careful the copies,
how complete the imitating serif,
how void my brain.
"She's been forging notes."
I whispered, "   ", for I could
not expose how the green ink lines
carved deep lines in my seeing.
Yes, I saw words like mine,
capital letters like mine,
deception, sorrow, mocking.

DON'T WORRY, LITTLE POEM

I won't write you and team us up in despair.
No iron shoes, no taut lines for you.
I, strafed and straitened, bow in the harness,
I shall let you go free.
No, you needn't accompany me.
Your beauty stands without me.
You, flinging an un-arrestable glance,
must not be bruised by the impatience
and haste of your pretentious mistress.

VESTIGIAL SUN

caught between two hills,
a pea in a crow's beak,
a ball bearing of flat sides,
too worn, too small,
a dropped amalgam.

Please don't roll away, little sun.
Don't blacken, wink out, vanish.
Stay, and change my black to gold.

Burn, little ball, burn bright
so our shadows can lengthen,
your kind glare lighting my alley.

FROM THE VIEWPOINT OF ONE WHO WAS SAD
A LOT

Dank gray-green at evening,
lightless behind opaque windows,
no promise of heat or touch,
no comfort in unhopeful eyes—

tonight I turn down an unfamiliar
street mistakenly, signal left and see it through,
shuttling along windows and wrought
iron inches from the window.
Rain comes down like moss in still water.

The porches in 30-year-old paint,
hardly spacious or inviting, wait in
empty light between dark and
darker evening, lifeless in
stolid and motionless mien.

If memory is livened by the present
sojourn through dank evening stall,
it can reach back through the sorrowful
screen of nights of last month, last
year and consider *what is warmth.*

GUARDIAN OF FLIGHT

What will the wind bring today?
I move ahead, as tentatively
as the first breeze graces me.
Tired, my sight dimmed, my compass
needle making no sweep, I recline.

What are these loose linens I wear?
Were they once a sail, bulging lobe
of a wilder wind, borne by the high
shoulders of a mast of yew?

I am that sail, a guardian of flight
embracing the powered air, riding water
and leaping up ridges: fighting whips
that lick and spit and could take us all down.

UNSEASONABLE PRUNING

Figwort, bramble twig,
bark and tender growing,
big root, twisted rig,
knotted shadow flowing.

Why amputate or try
to bare the splendid roots?
Dry, knurled plants will die
shorn of ancient roots.

THE TAP ROOT

Leave this poem unwritten.
Let its words lie underground
in the branch of a tap root—
the nurturing parent.

ACKNOWLEDGMENTS

Academy of the Heart and Mind: The Same Privacy, Out from the Epicenter, Basins of Sound, The Psyche in Waiting, and A Paean to Being Home
Amethyst Review: Basins of Sound, Out from the Epicenter, and The Same Privacy
Blue Moon Literary & Art Review: Red, The Pink Bar of Soap, and Auden Used a Laundry List
Eclectica Magazine: Said to a Drowned Daddy Longlegs
Eunoia Review: Legacy, Surrender, In the Glow of Having Been Obscure, Not Little Girls, The House, and Secret Coals
Iacoustic: Do You Want a Poem?, The Very Things Poetized, Sonnet After Lunch, Perfecting, and What is Virtue to One is Cardinal Sin to the Other
January Review: My Moon, My Full Moon, My Wallet of Aging, and Away from Speeding Laughter
Literary Yard: The Same Privacy
Poetic Diversity: Where I Have My Landmarks
POETiCA REViEW: I'd Never Title a Poem "Hope" and Go, and Feast Your Eyes
Taj Mahal Review: Hollows and Pockets

"Heartfelt gratitude must first be given to our brilliant, sensitive cousin Gayle Jansen Beede. She and our mother hummed along on the same creative frequency and always loved and appreciated each other. Gayle has tirelessly worked on this book, showing incredible dedication to our mother's work and memory. Without Gayle's thoughtful guidance and beautiful contributions this project would never have been realized. We are forever indebted to her.

We are also so very grateful to John Sibley Williams, who recognized our mother's gift and decided to represent us on this project. His remarkable insights and experience were reassuring during this process. He deftly navigated unknown territory for us and answered all questions with gentle confidence. His intelligent contributions were innumerable and greatly appreciated.
Our mother's teacher, Corita Kent, must also be acknowledged. She gave our mother full permission to create atypically. Her influence on our mother's paintings and writing was profound and lifelong.

And lastly, to our cousin Regine Wood, whose encouragement in every creative endeavor has been constant. Her early insights contributed greatly to this project and her love of poetry and the arts continue to inspire us."

—Camille Komine and Jane Hendrickson

Phoebe Marrall, orphaned at the age of nine, was a survivor of The Depression and of a grueling childhood. When she died in 2017 at the age of eighty-four, her daughters Jane Hendrickson and Camille Komine inherited hundreds of poems she had written. They remained unpublished during her lifetime but have posthumously been published in *Blue Moon Literary & Art Review, POETiCA REViEW, Eunoia Review, iacoustic, January Review, Eclectica Magazine, Amethyst Review, Literary Yard,* and elsewhere.

www.ingramcontent.com/pod-product-compliance
Lightning Source LLC
Chambersburg PA
CBHW021155090426
42740CB00008B/1106